Unofficial Harry Potter Cookbook

Harry Potter-Themed Recipes for Young Witches and Wizards

Ella Jade

Contents

Delve into your deepest memories of Hogwarts with these Harry Potter themed recipes. Recreate your favorite drinks and dishes from the Great Hall feasts, the Three Broomsticks Pub, and Mrs. Weasley's kitchen.

Start with a smooth Avocado Kedavra dip with some crunchy tortilla chips. While your guests eat, throw some Sickle Slices (fried zucchini sticks) into the oven. Dip them in some ranch when they're nice and crispy.

Move onto Quidditch Quesadillas for your main course. Dip them in sour cream and salsa. Your belly will be the size of a Bludger.

After you've filled your stomach, with almost no room left, you squeeze in some dessert because it l ooks so darn good.

Make a Chocolate Frogs Crockpot Cake and amaze your guests. They may have to roll home, but there's no such thing as bad publicity for a Harry

Potter party, right?

To ensure your success, we have a couple of Harry's hints to run by you. All the temperatures are in Fahrenheit. Don't burn your house down by accident as if you started a Fiendfyre.

Pretend you're McGonagall and use common sense. If the chicken isn't cooked after twenty minutes, put it in a bit longer. Be a Ravenclaw. Don't be a Hufflepuff and eat raw chicken.

Most dishes will serve at least two people, but kids eat different amounts so it's tough to put an exact number on it. If there are four chicken breasts, that's enough for four adults, or maybe two adults and four kids.

All the drinks are for young, Hogwarts students. They don't contain any alcohol. The act of brewing your Butterbeer and Felix Felicis will be fun enough. Possibly too much.

Prepare to have a magical time assembling,

cooking, and consuming these recipes. Who knows, maybe the experience will bring your magic powers to life. Dumbledore is waiting to send the letter. You just have to reignite the flame in your heart.

APPETIZERS & SNACKS

AVOCADO KEDAVRA DIP

Despite its name and green color, this dip will not kill you. It's actually very healthy while being super delicious. You'll have the energy to duel the meanest wizards.

INGREDIENTS

1 tbsp lime juice
1 tbsp chopped garlic
3 avocados
1 tsp paprika
pepper and salt to taste
¾ cup plain Greek yogurt

PREPARATION:

1. Add all items to a blender.
2. Blend until smooth.
3. Serve with veggies, pita bread, or crackers.

CARAMEL COBWEB DIP

This dip tastes like candy but is still very healthy. Definitely something you might find in a real-life Honeydukes.

INGREDIENTS

8 dates
4 tbsp coconut oil
½ cup almond milk
1 tsp vanilla extract
caramel sauce

PREPARATION:

1. Put all ingredients together in a food. processor and blend until smooth.
2. Drizzle caramel sauce on top.
3. Enjoy with fruit.

CENTAUR CHEESE BITES

Ronan is half man, half horse. These homemade cheese bites contain the same versatility, being half cracker, half delicious snack.

INGREDIENTS

1/3 tsp salt
1 3/4 cup shredded cheese
¼ cup chopped butter
¼ cup water
1 cup flour

PREPARATION:

1. Preheat oven to 375.
2. Put all except water into a food processor and blend until crumbly.
3. Pour mixture into a large bowl and slowly mix, adding a little bit of water at a time.
4. Once the dough no longer crumbles roll it out and cut into shapes of your choice.
5. Bake for 11 minutes or until browned.

COMMON-ROOM CORNUCOPIA

Who doesn't love a wide variety of flavors all at once? These stuffed croissants are a perfect movie night snack to enjoy on the couch surrounded by the ones you love.

INGREDIENTS

1 package of croissant rolls
1 green apple
8 slices of brie cheese
4 tbsp of hot and sweet mustard

PREPARATION:

1. Prepare the croissants per the instructions on the package.
2. Slice the green apple into 8 pieces.
3. Once croissants are done let them cool and slice a pocket into them.
4. Fill each croissant with an apple slice, a slice of brie and ½ tbsp of mustard.
5. Share with your family and enjoy!

DOBBY BREAD BISCUITS

Dobby was a very loyal and doting House Elf who loved to cook. These biscuits remind us of the loving relationship he had with Harry.

INGREDIENTS

1 tsp of minced garlic
3 tbsp melted butter
1 package of refrigerated flaky biscuits
½ cup parmesan cheese
½ tsp Italian seasoning

PREPARATION:

1. Preheat the oven to the temperature stated on the biscuit packaging.
2. Cut each raw biscuit into 6 pieces so you have little dough chunks.
3. Mix together all ingredients.
4. Add the dough chunks to the mixture and shake the bowl so pieces are coated.
5. Place 4-5 pieces of dough into each greased muffin compartment.
6. Bake until done and enjoy!

DIAGON ALLEY DAILY FRUITIES

Consider these a healthy version of Bertie Bott's Every Flavor Beans. Except these are always good flavors, fruit flavors to be exact.

INGREDIENTS

1/3 cup berries
1/3 cup fresh orange juice
4 tbsp gelatin
1 tbsp honey

PREPARATION:

1. Heat berries and juice in a pot on the stove.
2. Stir in honey.
3. Remove pot from heat and slowly mix in gelatin, stirring constantly.
4. Pour mix into a glass dish and put in the fried until set.
5. Cut into small cubes and enjoy.

DILLY WEED BISCUITS

Hogwarts is no place for boring. Your home should be the same. Use this fun recipe to spice up any cracker in your life, for when you need a little extra kick.

INGREDIENTS

1 package of ranch salad dressing mix
2.5 cups oyster crackers
½ cup canola oil
1 ½ tsp dill

PREPARATION:

1. Mix the oil, dressing mix and dill together in a bowl.
2. Put the crackers in a large bowl.
3. Pour the dressing mixture over the crackers.
4. Toss to ensure the crackers are coated.
5. Let sit for 1.5 hours before serving.

FLUFFY'S STICK

Fluffy is only put to sleep by the sound of music. We wonder if it would have worked if Harry, Ron, and Hermione had tried to distract him with this stick snack.

INGREDIENTS

6 long pretzel sticks
18 grapes
18 cubes of cheese
6 strawberries
peanut butter for dipping

PREPARATION:

1. Wash fruit.
2. Slide fruit and cheese onto the pretzel sticks.
3. Dip in peanut butter and enjoy.

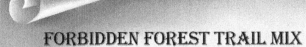

FORBIDDEN FOREST TRAIL MIX

Harry and his crew wander the Forbidden Forest way more often than they should. Which is technically never. Because it's forbidden. Anyway. Bet they wish they had this mix on them when they got cornered by Aragog's spider clan.

INGREDIENTS

½ cup M&Ms
½ cup raisins
½ cup peanuts
½ cup chopped dried apricots
½ cup dark chocolate chips

PREPARATION:

1. Mix all ingredients together.
2. Divide into baggies or containers for an easy on the go snack.

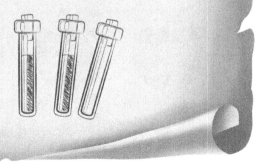

HEDWIG'S HEARTY FRUIT DIP

Hedwig was a sweet owl. Why not create a sweet dip in her honor? Pair this dip with freshly-sliced fruits for a yummy snack when you're feeling hungry.

INGREDIENTS

1 cup cream cheese
¾ cup of marshmallow cream
¾ cup fruit flavored yogurt
1 cup of cool whip

PREPARATION:

1. Use a potato masher or electric beaters to mix cream cheese and yogurt together.
2. Add marshmallow cream and cool whip to the mixture.
3. Dip your fruits and enjoy!

INVISIBLE CLOAK DIP

This super healthy dip is filled with broccoli, but you would never know because it tastes so good. Fool your family into eating healthy by cloaking the broccoli with your cooking skills.

INGREDIENTS

half a glass of prepared green pesto
2 cups broccoli
2 tbsp chopped garlic
1 tbsp lemon juice
¼ cup parmesan cheese
¼ cup ricotta cheese

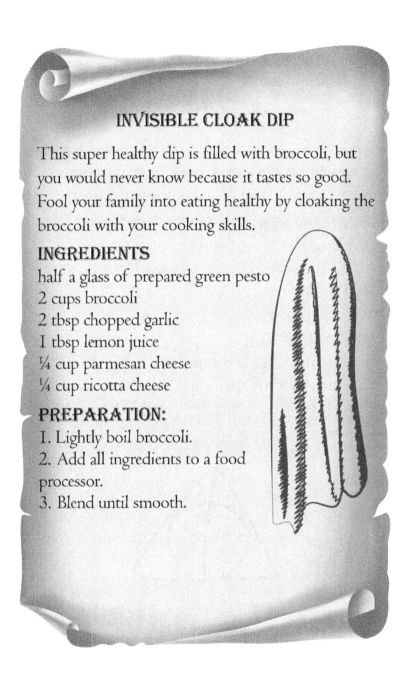

PREPARATION:

1. Lightly boil broccoli.
2. Add all ingredients to a food processor.
3. Blend until smooth.

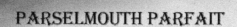

PARSELMOUTH PARFAIT

Looking for a delicious, but easy, afterschool snack? This one hits the spot. It won't break the glass and release a snake, though, so don't worry about that.

INGREDIENTS

1 cup vanilla Greek yogurt
1 1/3 cup unsweetened applesauce
2/3 cup granola
cinnamon to taste

PREPARATION:

1. Mix applesauce and nutmeg.
2. Spoon layers of applesauce, yogurt, and granola into a bowl.
3. Enjoy!

POPCORN PUKING PASTILLES

These popcorn treats would make George and Fred very jealous. With orange and purple varieties, you can still cure your (fake) illness.

INGREDIENTS

8 cups plain popped popcorn
1/3 cup corn syrup
3 tbsp butter
½ cup brown sugar
¼ cup dried apricots
¼ cup dried blueberries

PREPARATION:

1. Heat a pan over medium heat and prepare a bowl of cold water.
2. Mix together the syrup, butter and sugar in the pan.
3. Pour syrup over the popcorn.
4. Add apricots and blueberries.
5. Dip hands into cold water and scoop some popcorn mixture, press into a ball and place them onto a baking sheet, let sit and serve.

PROTEGO YOGURT POPS

This snack will protect you just like the shield charm. It can protect from the heat by cooling you down. It can protect you from excess sugars and dyes. /

INGREDIENTS

I tub fruit yogurt of your choice
I bag of pretzels

PREPARATION:

1. Spoon yogurt into an empty yogurt tray.
2. Stick pretzels into each cube of yogurt
3. Freeze for a few hours.
4. Remove from tray and enjoy!

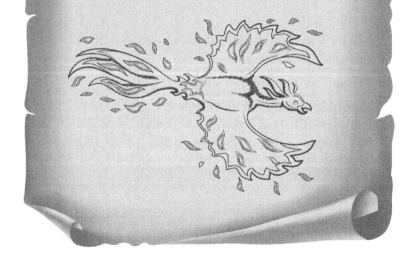

RON'S APPLE CHIPS

This recipe yields a lot of reward for your efforts. With a family as big as the Weasleys big recipes would always be a must. Enjoy these apple chips as an afterschool snack. But don't eat too many, dehydrated fruit can hurt your tummy.

INGREDIENTS

6 apples
cinnamon to taste

PREPARATION:

1. Preheat oven to 275.
2. Use an apple corer to remove the apple cores.
3. Slice the apples into thin slices.
4. Arrange on a baking sheet.
5. Bake slices for 2 hours, flipping once.

SICKLE SLICES

Harry always has lots of coins on him, and even more in his vault. These sickle slices will make you feel rich, even if they're not real money.

INGREDIENTS

salt to taste
oil
ranch seasoning
4 zucchini

PREPARATION:

1. Preheat oven to 225 degrees.
2. Chop zucchini into ¼ inch slices.
3. Toss zucchini slices in oil and coat with ranch seasoning and salt.
4. Bake for 1.5 hours until zucchini chips are browned and crispy.

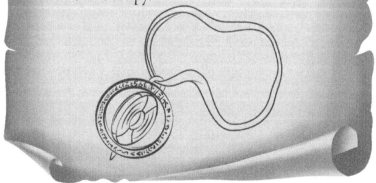

SPECKLED SNITCH ENERGY BALLS

These no-bake treats are great for a quick breakfast on the go. If you'd like to make them golden, simply use white chocolate chips. Once you eat these, you'll be flying fast. Just like Harry.

INGREDIENTS

1 ½ cup of rolled oats
1 scoop of protein powder (optional)
½ cup of nut butter
¼ cup semi-sweet chocolate chips
2 tbsp honey
*add in milk or water by the tbsp if you need more liquid, you will need more liquid if you add protein powder

PREPARATION:

1. Mix dry ingredients into peanut butter.
2. Add honey.
3. Stir intensely.
4. Add liquid as needed.
5. Roll mixture into 1 inch balls.
6. Cool in the fridge and eat!

UNICORN POOP DIP

If you look hard enough in the Forbidden Forest, you'd probably find unicorn poop. It would be pretty and smell like candy because unicorns are perfect.

INGREDIENTS

½ cup powdered sugar
¼ cup cream
½ cup marshmallow fluff
½ cup cream cheese
pink, purple, and blue food coloring
½ tsp vanilla extract
sprinkles

PREPARATION:

1. Mix powdered sugar with marshmallow fluff and cream cheese.
2. Add vanilla, cream, and a pinch of salt.
3. Divide dip into different bowls and add food coloring.
4. Swirl different color dips together in one big bowl and serve with fresh fruit.

MAINS AND SIDES

BATTERED PLIMPY NUGGETS

Luna didn't catch these fish, but they probably taste just as good. Serve these battered fish nuggets with veggies and rice, or amp up the British vibes with a side of chips (French fries).

INGREDIENTS

4 cod or haddock filets
4 tbsp parmesan cheese
1/3 tsp of salt
½ tsp of pepper
melted butter
2/3 cup panko breadcrumbs

PREPARATION:

1. Preheat oven to 375.
2. Cube the fish fillets into 1-inch pieces.
3. Mix cheese, salt, pepper, and breadcrumbs.
4. Dip fish cubes into melted butter and roll in breadcrumb mixture.
5. Place on a baking sheet and bake for 18-20 minutes.

BLUDGERS AND MASH

A carb-loaded comfort meal that would be great to eat after a long day at a Quidditch match.

INGREDIENTS

2 sausages
3 medium sized potatoes
¼ cup of milk
3 tbsp salted butter
1 red onion, sliced
¼ cup balsamic vinegar
1 cube of beef stock
1 cup of water

PREPARATION:

1. Put a pot of water on the stove.
2. Wash, peel, and chop your potatoes.
3. Gently slide the potatoes into the pot of water.
4. Bring the pot to a boil.
5. Boil potatoes until they are soft and tender.

Continued on next page.

BLUDGERS AND MASH

6. While potatoes are boiling heat a pan on medium heat.

7. Add sausages to the pan and fry until fully cooked through.

8. Remove from the pan, cover, and place aside.

9. Drain the potatoes.

10. Add 2 tbsp butter and milk to the potatoes.

11. Mash with a potato masher until smooth.

12. Cover and set aside.

13. Heat 1tbsp of butter in the pan.

14. Fry onions until golden.

15. Add in balsamic vinegar and stock.

16. Add water and stir until gravy is formed.

17. Pile the sausages on top of your mashed potatoes and top with gravy.

BUBBLE-HEAD BROCCOLI SALAD

You won't be able to breathe underwater like Cedric Diggory during the Triwizard Tournament, but you will come out a winner. This salad is a treat for the whole family.

INGREDIENTS

¾ cup bacon bits
½ cup craisins
1/3 cup chopped red onion
2 chopped broccoli crowns
1 tsp white sugar
¾ cup mayonnaise
1.5 tbsp red wine vinegar

PREPARATION:

1. Mix broccoli, onion, bacon and craisins together in a large bowl.
2. Mix mayonnaise, vinegar, and sugar together in a separate bowl.
3. Pour mayonnaise mixture into large bowl, mix together and enjoy.

BUTTERMILK Q'WAFFLES

There's no doubt Harry always had a good breakfast before a Quidditch match, why shouldn't you? Nothing beats buttermilk. Even Beaters.

INGREDIENTS

a pinch of salt
½ tsp baking powder
½ tsp baking soda
I cup flour
I egg
2 tbsp melted butter
I cup buttermilk

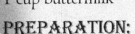

PREPARATION:

1. Mix the egg, buttermilk, and butter together in a large bowl.
2. Add in the salt, baking powder, baking soda and flour until the batter is smooth.
3. Pour a half cup of batter into a greased waffle iron and cook until golden brown.

CHAMBER OF SECRETS CASSEROLE

You never know what you might find in the Chamber of Secrets. This casserole is the same. Equal parts health and excitement it will keep everyone in the family happy, and out of Tom Riddle's grasp.

INGREDIENTS

½ cup chopped onion
1.5 pounds ground turkey
3 cups of frozen tater tots
2 cups frozen mixed veggies
1 can corn niblets
½ cup milk
1 can condensed cream of broccoli soup
1 can condensed cream of chicken soup

PREPARATION:

1. Preheat oven to 350.
2. Fry onions, turkey and veggies in a large pan over medium heat.
3. Mix soup cans and milk together in a small bowl.
Continued on the next page.

30

CHAMBER OF SECRETS CASSEROLE II

PREPARATION:

4. Pour meat mixture into a greased casserole dish.
5. Pour soup mixture on top.
6. Top with tater tots.
7. Bake for about an hour or until golden brown.
8. Cut into squares and enjoy!

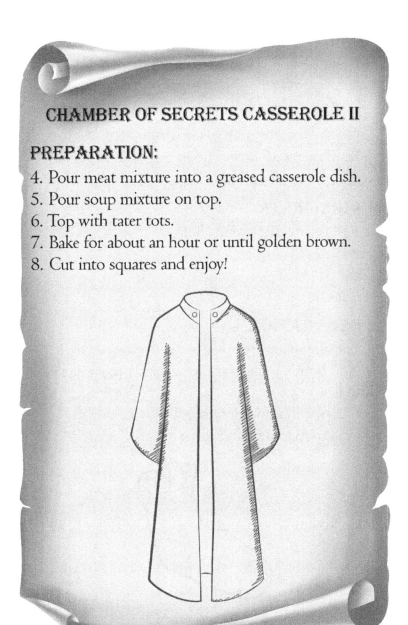

GOBLIN GOOP

Goblin's love gold. They also love hidden treasure. This easy macaroni and cheese upgrade will send you on a ride all through Gringotts.

INGREDIENTS

1 package macaroni and cheese
butter
milk
4 hot dogs

PREPARATION:

1. Boil the macaroni.
2. Add butter, milk, and cheese packet to strained noodles.
3. Chop up hotdogs into small pieces.
4. Add to macaroni and mix.

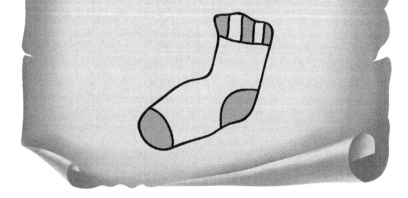

GRINGOTTS PB & BANANA BUTTY

This sandwich looks like gold, and it tastes like four stars! Feel an exhilaration similar to Harry's first time entering the vaults when this yummy meal hits your tummy.

INGREDIENTS

2 slices of toast or bread
1 banana, sliced
1/8 cup of peanut butter
1 tbsp mini chocolate chips
1 tbsp honey
a pinch of cinnamon

PREPARATION:

1. Mix the peanut butter, honey, cinnamon and chocolate chips together.
2. Spread peanut butter mixture onto both slices of bread.
3. Place sliced banana pieces onto the peanut butter on one piece of bread.
4. Put the other piece of bread onto the banana slices. Cut in half and enjoy!

GRYFFINDOR CUPS

Craving a burger but don't really feel like going through all the trouble of a home-made patty? Ron, Hermione, and Harry have a magical solution for you.

INGREDIENTS

1 tube of refrigerated biscuits (buttermilk or flaky)
1 ½ tbsp brown sugar
¼ cup ketchup
3 tbsp of cream cheese
2 tsp Worcestershire sauce
1 tbsp honey Dijon mustard
1 small package of ground beef
1 package of Kraft singles

PREPARATION:

1. Preheat the oven based on biscuit package recommendation.
2. Heat a pan on medium and fry up the ground beef.
3. Drain the liquid.
   Continue on the next page.

GRYFFINDOR CUPS

PREPARATION:

4. Add ketchup, mustard, Worcestershire sauce, and brown sugar.
5. Separate biscuits and place into greased muffin tins.
6. Scoop ground beef mixture into each cup.
7. Bake until cooked.
8. Remove cups from the oven and top with a slice of cheese.
9. Bake again until melted.
10. Let cool and enjoy.

HAGRID'S BREAKFAST

Ever wonder how Hagrid got so big and strong?
Well, he's half giant. But even so, a healthy, nutritious
breakfast is always key.

INGREDIENTS

1 tbsp honey
a dash of cinnamon
1 tsp ground flaxseed
1 cup quick oats
1.5 tbsp nut butter
2 cups lightly salted water

PREPARATION:
1. Boil the water in a small pot.
2. Add the oats and simmer until fully cooked.
3. Stir in all other ingredients.
4. Transfer oatmeal into bowl(s).
5. Enjoy with a side of fruit.

HOGWARTS HAM AND HASH

This easy recipe is perfect after a long week, being equal parts easy and delicious. This meal is inspired by the long tables in Hogwarts and a family-style eating experience.

INGREDIENTS

6 carrots
I yellow onion
1.5 tbsp brown sugar
¾ tsp horseradish
I tbsp olive oil

7 medium sized potatoes
I small cooked ham
¾ tsp lemon zest
½ cup orange juice
Salt and pepper

PREPARATION:

I. Preheat oven to 425.
2. Toss potatoes and carrots with oil, salt, and pepper.
3. Roast veggies for 27 minutes.
4. Mix orange juice, brown sugar, lemon zest, and horseradish together.
5. Slice ham and place slices on top of roasted veggies.
6. Pour orange juice mixture on top.
7. Bake for 10 minutes.

HUFFLEPUFFS IN A BLANKET

A Harry Potter twist on a classic comfort meal. Serve these with honey Dijon mustard for a magical explosion of flavor.

INGREDIENTS

1 package of croissant rolls
8 hot dogs
4 tbsp red pepper jelly

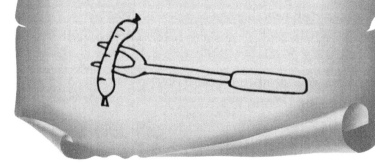

PREPARATION:

1. Divide the croissant rolls on a baking sheet.
2. Spread red pepper jelly onto the croissant dough.
3. Roll hot dogs into the croissants.
4. Bake per the instructions on the package of the croissants.
5. Let croissants cool and cut into two.
6. Serve with mustard and enjoy!

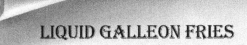

LIQUID GALLEON FRIES

They're actually cheese fries, but that's as good as liquid gold, don't you think? This is a great treat for awesome kids who have proven to be exemplary.

INGREDIENTS

¼ tsp garlic powder
½ tsp onion powder
I package of frozen fries
I ¼ cup of condensed cheddar cheese soup
¼ cup of milk

PREPARATION:

1. Bake fried per the instructions on the package.
2. Combine soup mix, garlic and onion powder, and milk in a small pot.
3. Once fries are done, drizzle cheese mix on top.
4. Serve to your family and enjoy.

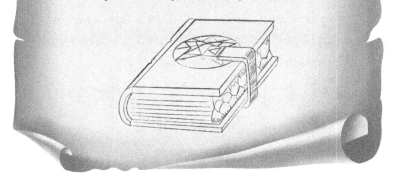

39

MAGIC MARMALADE MOCK-OS

Tacos for breakfast? Why not. Just make them sweet. The Three Broomsticks should add this to their menu. They'd be selling out day and night.

INGREDIENTS
2 tbsp peanut butter
2 tbsp marmalade
handful of strawberries
handful of blueberries
2 crushed graham crackers
2 slices of white bread
1 tbsp honey

PREPARATION:
1. Use a cookie cutter to cut bread into a circular shape.
2. Squish bread to make it flat.
3. Spread peanut butter and marmalade on bread.
4. Chop strawberries, sprinkle onto the bread with blueberries and crackers.
5. Fold up and top with honey.

MUDBLOOD MAC 'N' CHEESE

Mudblood children are no strangers to Muggle food since they were raised by none other than Muggles. This classic staple is great for a rainy day.

INGREDIENTS

1 ½ tbsp melted butter
1 ¼ cup cubed Velveeta
2.5 cups elbow noodles
1 ¾ cups milk
2 ¼ cups shredded cheese
breadcrumbs

PREPARATION:

1. Boil macaroni until al dente.
2. Mix all ingredients (except for breadcrumbs) in with the noodles.
3. Pour into slow cooker and cook on low for 3 hours.
4. Halfway through top with additional cheese and breadcrumbs.

NEVILLE'S GRANDMA'S FRUIT CURRY

Eating foods from across the world is always exciting. Neville's Grandma is always looking out for him. This curry is sweet and delicious giving you a grandmotherly type of comfort when eating. Serve with rice.

INGREDIENTS

1 yellow onion
1 large can fruit medley
½ cup apple or orange juice
3 tbsp curry powder
4 chicken breasts, chopped
salt and pepper
1 tbsp flour

PREPARATION:

1. Fry the chicken in a pan, season with salt and pepper.
2. Set chicken aside.
3. Fry onions in the pan with curry powder.

Continued on the next page.

NEVILLE'S GRANDMA'S FRUIT CURRY

PREPARATION:

4. Pour juice and the juices from the fruit can into the pan.
5. Add flour as needed to thicken the sauce.
6. Add remaining curry powder, chicken and fruit.
7. Simmer until chicken is thoroughly coated.
8. Plate and serve.

NEWT'S NACHOS

This comfort food has a little bit of everything you need, just like the nastily exhausting wizarding tests. These nachos have a lot less stress involved though.

INGREDIENTS

1 bag tortilla chips	1 can corn
1 cup black beans	1 tomato
2 cups shredded cheese	2 tbsp chopped cilantro
½ red onion	1 jalapeno
Salsa	Sour cream

PREPARATION:

1. Preheat the oven to 400 degrees.
2. Spread tortilla chips on a baking sheet.
3. Chop tomato and onion, slice jalapeno.
4. Load beans, tomato, onion, jalapeno, corn, cheese, and cilantro onto chips.
5. Bake in the oven for 5 minutes or until all cheese has melted.

PATRONUS PIZZA

A pizza masquerading as a breakfast food? This is a magical land. Anything is allowed. Use your Patronus to ward off angry parents when they realize you're having pizza for breakfast (but then offer them a slice)!

INGREDIENTS

4 tbsp bacon bits
1 bag of shredded cheese mix
5 eggs
1 package of prepared pizza dough
1.5 tbsp olive oil

PREPARATION:

1. Preheat oven based on dough package instructions.
2. Roll out dough onto a pre-greased pan.
3. Brush the dough with olive oil.
4. Bake until the dough is lightly browned.
5. While dough is baking whisk the eggs together and scramble them slightly in a medium pan.
6. Remove crust from oven.

Continued on the next page.

PATRONUS PIZZA

PREPARATION:

7. Put eggs onto the crust.

8. Top with bacon bits and cheese.

9. Put pizza back into the oven and bake until the cheese is melted.

10. Slice the pizza and enjoy once cooled.

PEANUT BUTTER AND JELLY WANDS

We know we're not supposed to play with our food, but sometimes it just can't be helped. This fun way to eat a sandwich will help you explore your magical abilities.

INGREDIENTS

2 slices of toast or bread
2 tbsp jam
2 tbsp peanut butter
a handful of grapes

PREPARATION:

1. Smear your peanut butter on one slice of bread and your jam on the other.
2. Slap the two pieces of bread together.
3. Cut the bread lengthwise, with one side being ¾ of the bread wide.
4. Cut the two pieces in half.
5. Slide the bigger squares onto a skewer first, followed by the smaller squares.
6. Top off your wand with grapes, use the bigger ones first to create a tapered wand shape.

PETTIGREW PITA

A healthy but yummy sandwich alternative. You'll be stuck on this meal, just like Peter Pettigrew was stuck on Ron. You might not see the sandwich on the Marauder's map though.

INGREDIENTS

1 pita, whole wheat preferred
½ apple, sliced thin
½ banana, sliced thin
2 tbsp peanut butter
1 tsp honey

PREPARATION:

1. Cut the pita bread in half to form two pockets.
2. Spread peanut butter inside both halves.
3. Slide apple and banana slices into the pockets.
4. Drizzle with honey.
5. Eat and enjoy!

POLTERGEIST POTATO SALAD

It's unknown whether ghosts can hear or not, but it's plausible the Hogwarts permanent residents would enjoy this recipe as much as you will.

INGREDIENTS

1 tbsp pickle juice
3 tbsp honey Dijon mustard
4 hardboiled eggs
½ cup mayonnaise
Salt and pepper to taste
½ yellow onion
5 medium red potatoes
4 dill pickles

PREPARATION:

1. Boil potatoes until soft.
2. Finely chop the onion, eggs, and pickles.
3. Cube the boiled potatoes once they've cooled.
4. Mix mayonnaise, mustard, pickle juice, salt, and pepper together.
5. Combine potatoes, onion, egg, pickles and mayonnaise mixture.

PRIVET DRIVE PITA POCKET

This is a great meal to use when you have leftover chicken in the house or you're just looking to create something that looks like Aunt Petunia's outfits. This chicken salad pita is bright and fun though, unlike her.

INGREDIENTS

2 tbsp craisins
¼ cup chopped green apple
2 tbsp mayonnaise
A pinch of salt
1 pita
¼ cup sliced celery
½ cup pulled chicken
2 pinches onion powder
½ tsp lemon juice

PREPARATION:

1. Wash and chop the veggies and fruit.
2. Cut pita in half to create 2 pockets.
3. Mix ingredients (except for pita) together in a bowl.
4. Stuff pita halves with chicken salad mixture.

PUMPKIN CURRY LENTIL SOUP

A warm bowl of soup keeps the Death Eaters away.
Or so they say. Enjoy this Hogwarts flavored soup
on a cool day. It usually ends up the color of
Hermione's hair!

INGREDIENTS

½ can pureed pumpkin
½ cup yellow lentils
1 can coconut milk
1 cup vegetable stock
1 tbsp Thai curry paste
3 tbsp curry powder

PREPARATION:

1. Put all items into a slow cooker.
2. Cook on high for 2 hours.
3. Use a hand blender to blend soup into a puree.
4. Serve and enjoy.

QUIDDITCH QUESADILLAS

A tortilla shell must be around the size of a Bludger. Here's another hearty meal to prepare you for all the activities at Hogwarts.

INGREDIENTS

2 large flour tortillas
1 tsp minced cilantro
½ avocado
¼ cup shredded cheese
2 tbsp homemade salsa
Sour cream for serving

PREPARATION:

1. Heat a large pan over medium heat.
2. Peel and slice the avocado half.
3. Place one tortilla in pan and sprinkle cheese on top, wait for cheese to melt.
4. Add cilantro, salsa, and avocado.
5. Top with the other quesadilla and cook on both sides until golden brown.
6. Cut into 6 pieces and serve with sour cream.

SORTING HATS

Hummus, Avocado, Tomato, and Shallots. What more could one ask for on a sandwich? Now if only it could sort you into your Hogwarts house.

INGREDIENTS

1 large tomato
1 shallot
1 avocado
A pinch of pepper and salt
3 tbsp of hummus
6 slices of toast

PREPARATION:

1. Slice the tomato and avocado, chop the shallot.
2. Spread avocado over 3 slices of toast and hummus over remaining 3 slices of toast.
3. Top one half with the veggies.
4. Turn into sandwiches.
5. Cut each sandwich in 2 and enjoy!

SPICY SLYTHERIN STICKS

It's always been a mystery why Draco was such a bully. If he'd had these sweet potato fries to snack on, he probably would have been kinder. Hopefully he finds this recipe. Does anyone have his e-mail?

INGREDIENTS

Pinch of cinnamon
2 tbsp olive oil
½ tsp chili powder
¾ tsp garlic powder
½ tsp ground pepper
¾ tsp curry powder
¼ tsp salt
3 sweet potatoes

PREPARATION:

1. Preheat oven to 425 degrees.
2. Wash and peel the potatoes.
3. Cut potatoes into ½ inch wide fries
4. Toss with olive oil and spices.
5. Spread on a non-stick baking sheet.
6. Bake for 15-20 minutes, turning once.

STUFFED HUFFLEPUFF BARRELS

The Hufflepuff common room is guarded by barrels. Do you know what's inside of them? Obviously these things. But these stuffed peppers are filled with yummy goodness and topped with crispy cheese.

INGREDIENTS

2 red peppers, tops cut off
I package ground meat
I tomato, chopped
I yellow onion, chopped

I cup prepared rice
I can corn
I package taco spice
½ cup shredded cheese

PREPARATION:

1. Preheat oven to 375.
2. Fry onions and ground meat in a pan on medium heat, add taco seasoning.
3. Add rice, corn, tomato to pan and mix.
4. Spoon mixture into red peppers.
5. Top with shredded cheese.
6. Bake in the oven for I5 minutes or until cheese is golden and pepper is softened.
7. Save remaining mixture for another time or eat separately.

THESTRAL TURKEY WRAPS

These wraps can be seen by anyone, not just those who have seen death. They taste yummy and are sure to be a hit amongst you and all your favorite magical creatures.

INGREDIENTS

2 tortilla wraps
2 tbsp mayonnaise
4 slices deli turkey
2 tbsp mustard
1 sliced tomato
½ cup shredded carrot

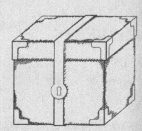

PREPARATION:

1. Spread mayonnaise and mustard on both tortilla wraps.
2. Add turkey, carrot, and tomato to wrap.
3. Roll up each tortilla.
4. Cut into 4 pieces and enjoy.

THREE BROOMSTICKS TACO BOWL

Tacos are yummy, but they can be super messy. These taco bowls encompass Hermione's love for adventure as well as her rigid self-control. It's a flavorful ride, but the mess is well contained.

INGREDIENTS

lime wedge

1 can of corn

½ pound ground beef

2 tbsp sour cream

½ avocado

cilantro lime rice

12 cherry tomatoes

taco seasoning

½ cup shredded cheese

2 tbsp chopped red onion

PREPARATION:

1. Prepare rice per package instructions.
2. Heat a large pan on medium high and cook ground beef, adding taco seasoning.
3. Chop cherry tomatoes into halves, avocado into chunks, drain corn.
4. Squeeze lime wedge into sour cream and mix.
5. Top rice with veggies, cheese, and sour cream.

TRANSFIGURATION SANDWICH

Is it pizza? A sandwich? Garlic bread? It's all three. Magic adheres to few rules and you shouldn't either. Enjoy this scrumptious meal on days you just want a little bit of everything.

INGREDIENTS

¼ cup pasta or pizza sauce
4 slices of garlic bread
cheese to cover all four slices of bread
pepperoni slices

PREPARATION:

1. Heat the garlic bread in a frying pan over medium heat.
2. Spread sauce on one side of each slice of bread.
3. Top with cheese and pepperoni and form sandwiches.
4. Toast on the pan until the cheese is melted.
5. Cut sandwiches in half and enjoy.

TRIWIZARD SALAD

Three fruits are just as powerful as three wizards when you put them together in the right way. Your tastebuds will be ready to defeat the meanest of dragons after having this meal!

INGREDIENTS

¾ cup cream cheese
1 tsp ground ginger
4 cups raspberries
8 nectarines
2 cups blueberries
½ cup sugar
2 tsp lemon juice

PREPARATION:

1. Wash fruits and slice the nectarines.
2. Set berries aside and put nectarines in a large bowl.
3. Coat nectarines with sugar, lemon, and ginger.
4. Put nectarines into the fridge for an hour.
5. Drain the juice from the nectarine mixture into a bowl with the cream cheese.

Continued on the next page.

TRIWIZARD SALAD

PREPARATION:

6. Mix the two together.

7. Combine berries with nectarines and serve the salad with the cream cheese mix.

VERITASERUM VEGGIE MELT

This delicious veggie melt will tickle your tastebuds so much you will need to defy the Ministry of Magic by telling the truth about this recipe.

INGREDIENTS

4 slices of bread
¼ cup mayonnaise
1 tsp chopped garlic
1 chopped onion
½ cup chopped mushrooms
½ cup shredded cheese
½ chopped red pepper
1 tbsp olive oil

PREPARATION:

1. Preheat the oven to 400 degrees.
2. Toss veggies in oil and roast in the oven for 15 minutes.
3. While veggies roast, mix mayonnaise and garlic.
4. Coat bread slices with mayonnaise mixture.
5. Remove veggies from oven and set oven to broil.
Continued on the next page.

VERITASERUM VEGGIE MELT

PREPARATION:

6. Divide veggies onto bread slices and top with shredded cheese.
7. Broil in oven until cheese is crispy on top.
8. Let cool and enjoy.

WAFFLE-WITCHES

Employ your magic skills as you turn your lunch sandwich into a waffle look-alike. Who would've thought?

INGREDIENTS

4 slices of whole wheat toast
4 slices of turkey meat
3 tbsp of cream cheese
a pinch of pepper
2 tbsp cranberry sauce
½ tbsp maple syrup
1 tbsp melted butter

PREPARATION:

1. Mix the cream cheese, pepper, cranberry sauce, and maple syrup together.
2. Spread onto all pieces of bread.
3. Top two slices of bread with turkey.
4. Turn bread into sandwiches.
5. Spread butter onto warm waffle iron.
6. Press sandwiches in the waffle iron until golden brown.

DESSERT

BERTIE BOTT'S EVERY FLAVOR TRAIL MIX

Enjoy every type of flavor emitting from this trail mix. Don't worry though, we left out the gross ones.

INGREDIENTS
1 package of jellybeans
2 cups of Lucky Charms
1 cup of M&M's
1 cup roasted nuts of your choice

PREPARATION:
1. Add all ingredients to a large bowl.
2. Mix thoroughly.
3. Enjoy your surprise.

BUTTERBEER COOKIES

A spin on the most popular Harry Potter drink of all time. These soft and chewy cookies should become a staple in the Gryffindor common room.

INGREDIENTS

I egg
½ cup sugar
½ tsp vanilla
I I/3 cup flour
½ package butterscotch
   pudding

½ cup brown sugar
½ cup butter
½ tsp salt
½ tsp baking soda
½ cup butterscotch chips
½ cup chocolate chips

PREPARATION:

1. Preheat oven to 375.
2. Mix sugars, egg, and vanilla.
3. Mix salt, pudding mix, and baking soda together before pouring in with the sugar mixture and mix.
4. Slowly add flour while mixing.
5. Spoon in chips and mix thoroughly.
6. Let dough chill in the fridge for I0-I5 minutes.
7. Spoon onto a baking sheet and bake for 9 minutes.

CAULDRON CAKE

Not just for witches. It's one of Harry's favorites! It might just be yours too.

INGREDIENTS

1 package of devil's food cake mix
2 chocolate pudding cups
canola oil per the amount on the cake mix
eggs per the amount on the cake mix
½ cup of sour cream
water per the amount on the cake mix
tub of your preferred icing
green food coloring

PREPARATION:

1. Preheat the oven to 325.
2. Grease muffin trays.
3. Mix cake mix with wet ingredients.
4. Pour batter into muffin tins.
5. Bake for 20 minutes or until a toothpick comes out with no batter.
6. Mix green food colouring into icing.
7. Ice cupcakes once cooled.
8. Enjoy your cauldron cakes.

CHOCOLATE FROGS CROCKPOT CAKE

Luckily, this won't jump away from you. Turn the famous chocolate frogs into an easy cake to enjoy with your friends!

INGREDIENTS

½ package of chocolate pudding mix
½ package of cake mix
1 cup of chocolate chips
1 large egg
2.5 tbsp oil
¾ cup of water
1 cup of milk

PREPARATION:

1. Mix the cake mix with the egg, water, and oil until thoroughly mixed.
2. Pour cake mix into the slow cooker.
3. Mix pudding mix and milk together.
4. Add choc-chips and let sit for 1 minute.
5. Pour pudding mix on top of the cake mixture.
6. Cook on high for 3-4 hours and then enjoy your cake!

HARRY'S HAYSTACKS

It's no secret that Harry has a sweet tooth. These haystacks combine sticky sweet goodness with the satisfying crunch of potato chips all in one go.

INGREDIENTS

6 cups of potato sticks
¾ cup butterscotch chips
1 ¼ cup peanut butter
caramel sauce

PREPARATION:

1. Put butterscotch chips and peanut butter into a microwave safe bowl.
2. Warm until melted through and stir together.
3. Stir in potato sticks.
4. Scoop out mixture with a tablespoon and plop onto a baking sheet.
5. Dollop some caramel sauce on top.
6. Place in the fridge or freezer until set.

MAGICAL FAIRY TOAST

Unicorns and fairies will gather when you eat this beautiful and tasty, magical toast.

INGREDIENTS

3 tbsp fruit jam
3 tbsp pink buttercream frosting
3 tbsp blue buttercream frosting
3 slices of toast
sprinkles

PREPARATION:

1. Spread jam onto each piece of toast.
2. Spread 1 tbsp of each frosting color onto toast, mixing colors together slightly.
3. Top with as many sprinkles as you'd like.

NIMBUS 2001

A broomstick as a treat? Say no more. Your tastebuds will be zooming around the quidditch field with excitement.

INGREDIENTS

large pretzel rods (as many as you'd like)
1 cup of granola
1.5 cups semi-sweet chocolate chips
regular sized pretzel rods

PREPARATION:

1. Melt the chocolate chips in a microwave safe container.
2. Dip the pretzel rods into the chocolate.
3. Stick regular sized pretzels around the end of the large pretzel rod.
4. Sprinkle granola onto the rest of the exposed chocolate.
5. Lay broomsticks on a waxed paper sheet until they are set.
6. Store in the fridge.

PEPPERMINT TOAD COOKIES

A wonderful holiday dessert you can enjoy with your family. This recipe emits coziness and happiness, like when Ron and harry opened gifts together Christmas morning.

INGREDIENTS

¼ cup sour cream

pinch of salt

pinch of baking soda

½ cup sugar

2 drops blue food coloring

1 tsp mint extract

1 egg

¼ cup soft butter

½ pouch vanilla pudding mix

1 cup flour

9 drops green food coloring

¾ cup chocolate chips

PREPARATION:

1. Preheat oven to 375.
2. Mix sugar and butter together.
3. Add pudding, egg, and sour cream.
4. Mix flour, baking soda, and salt together in a small, separate bowl.
5. Pour dry ingredients in with the wet ingredients while mixing, then add food coloring.

Continued on the next page.

PEPPERMINT TOAD COOKIES

PREPARATION:

6. Place tablespoon sized balls of dough onto a baking sheet.
7. Bake for 11 minutes.
8. Let cool and enjoy.

POLYJUICE JELLIES

Let's make some edible Polyjuice potions! Who doesn't love Jell-O? This fun party treat puts an extra delicious spin on a regular jelly dessert. Serve with whipped cream for extra fun.

INGREDIENTS

1 cup of canned pineapple juice
1 pouch of Jell-O, any flavor

PREPARATION:

1. Add one cup of warm water to your Jell-O mix.
2. Add cup of cold pineapple juice.
3. Pour mixture into tiny ketchup cups.
4. Let sit in the fridge.
5. Enjoy!

PYGMY PUFF POP

A hot summer day calls for a nice cool treat. These pops will keep you full while cooling you down, filled with healthy ingredients to keep the adults happy! It's a win, win!

INGREDIENTS

4 bananas
8 popsicle sticks
1 cup fruit yogurt of your choice
1.5 cups Fruity Pebbles cereal

PREPARATION:

1. Peel bananas and cut them in half.
2. Put bananas onto popsicle sticks.
3. Dip bananas into yogurt.
4. Dip bananas into cereal.
5. Place on waxed paper.
6. Freeze.
7. Enjoy once frozen.

RAVENCLAW CRISPS

Sweet and salty all in one bite. Diversity in a snack links well to a Ravenclaw's creativity. Their wisdom and wit doesn't limit them from having a little fun!

INGREDIENTS

1 cup semi-sweet chocolate chips
6 cups original flavored potato chips
2 tsp shortening

PREPARATION:

1. Mix chocolate chips and shortening in a microwave safe bowl.
2. Microwave until melted and smooth.
3. Lay chips out on a baking sheet.
4. Drizzle with chocolate.
5. Put into the fridge until chocolate hardens.

TIME-TURNER TREACLE TART

This tart will take you back in time.
Its sticky sweetness will remind you of early
childhood and make you feel warm inside. It was
one of Harry's favorite treats!

INGREDIENTS

1.5 tbsp melted butter
1.5 tbsp lemon juice
Zest of 1 lemon
1/3 cup cream
¾ cup golden syrup
1 medium egg
¾ cup breadcrumbs
1 pie crust

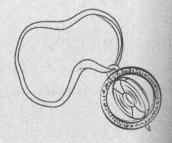

PREPARATION:

1. Poke holes into the pie crust and preheat oven to
375.
2. Mix lemon juice, zest, cream, syrup, egg,
breadcrumbs, and butter.
3. Spoon mixture into pie crust.
4. Bake for 38 minutes or until pie is lightly
browned.

WITCHES HATS

Why should Harry get all the glory when he wouldn't have gotten anywhere without Hermione? This yummy recipe celebrates all the awesome witches out there!

INGREDIENTS

1 package brownie mix
12 Hershey kisses
eggs
oil
water

PREPARATION:

1. Preheat oven to 375.
2. Pour brownie mix into a bowl.
3. Add in wet ingredients as stated on the box of your chosen mix.
4. Mix batter together until smooth.
5. Pour into a greased pan.
6. Bake for 30 minutes.
7. Quickly remove from oven and press kisses into the brownie at 1-inch intervals, cut and serve.

DRINKS AND POTIONS
ACCIO APPLE

Summon all the apples to your yard. This charming, fall treat of a drink will have you humming Halloween tunes in September. One sip, and you'll be surrounded by pumpkins faster than Harry can his Firebolt.

INGREDIENTS

4 ounces apple juice
1 ounce of ginger ale
¼ tsp cinnamon
1 tsp lemon juice

PREPARATION:

1. Rim the glass with a mixture of cinnamon and sugar.
2. Pour in your concoction.
3. Place a thin slice of apple on the rim as a garnish.
4. Cuddle by the fire and take a sip.

BELLATRIX'S BELLINI

Bellatrix was an evil woman. This helped her know how to make a mean drink. Sorry, just use Silencio now. Try her peach Bellini and forgive all her sins in an instant. It's easy, fresh, and delicious.

INGREDIENTS

3 peaches
3 cups sparkling water
1 oz simple syrup
ice

PREPARATION:

1. Add a cup of ice to your food processor.
2. Cut up fresh, frozen, or canned peaches and add to the mix.
3. Pour three cups of sparkling water.
4. Add an ounce of sugar water (simple syrup).
5. Blend.
6. Rim champagne flutes with sugar and pour in your concoction.
7. Garnish with a peach slice.

THE BURROW'S MIGHTY ORANGE JUICE

Molly Weasley always treated Harry so well. Almost more than her own children at times. Give yourself that same love with some orange juice worthy of breakfast at The Burrow.

INGREDIENTS

4 oranges
lemon zest
sugar

PREPARATION:

1. Smack four oranges on the table.
2. Cut them in half. Squeeze them with a juicer.
3. For less pulp/juicy bits, run it through a strainer
4. Rim the glass with a mixture of lemon zest and sugar.
5. Pour in your juice.
6. Scream at the freshness.

DUMBLEDORE'S DROP

Dumbledore loved lemon drops. Enjoy this refreshing spin on traditional lemonade for a hot summer's day.

INGREDIENTS

5 cups of water
¾ cup of white sugar
I cup lemon juice
I lemon
I cucumber, chopped
Optional: 10 fresh mint leaves

PREPARATION:

1. Add lemon juice, half of the cucumber, sugar and (optional) 5 mint leaves into a pot.
2. Cook over medium heat until the sugar is dissolved.
3. Strain the cucumber and mint (if used) from the rest of the mixture, pouring the liquid into a pitcher.
4. Slice up the lemon (ask an adult for help).
5. Add the rest of the ingredients to the pitcher.
6. Let the drink chill in the fridge for a few hours.
7. Pour and enjoy.

FELIX FELICIS

Ever wanted to try something but you were too afraid to fail? Remove that feat with Felix Felicis. This liquid luck will bring you the courage to try something you've always wanted to try. Yes, we're both thinking of skydiving.

INGREDIENTS

1 tbsp edible gold glitter
½ cup peach juice
½ cup pineapple juice
½ cup Sprite
3 slices of pineapple

PREPARATION:

1. Place ½ cup peach juice, ½ cup pineapple juice, ½ cup Sprite, two slices of pineapple, and a pinch of glitter in a blender. Mix until smooth.
2. Rim the glass with glitter if you're daring and would like sparkles on your face. Garnish with the last pineapple slice.

GILLYWATER

After drinking a sweet drink it's important to replenish your body with hydration. Gillywater is a fun spin on boring old water, providing you with yumminess that will keep you coming back for more.

INGREDIENTS

water – still or carbonated
5 cucumber slices
2 drops of lime juice

PREPARATION:

1. Wash your cucumber.
2. Carefully slice (or ask an adult for help) 5 slices of cucumber.
3. Add cucumber slices to a glass or bottle.
4. Squeeze two drops of lime from a lime wedge or bottle.
5. Enjoy your tasty hydration.

GINNY'S SPICY MARGARITAS

Ginny will grow up to make the best spicy margaritas. I just know it. Her red hair, her gentle nature, she's bound to love a good hint of spice to balance her sugar.

INGREDIENTS

3 oz lime juice
1 oz simple syrup
1 oz orange Fanta
salt
lime zest
jalapenos

PREPARATION:

1. Mix salt and lime zest. Use a lime slice to coat the rim then press in the salt mixture.
2. In a shaker glass, add ice, 3 oz lime juice, 1 oz simple syrup, 1 oz orange Fanta, and chopped up jalapenos.
3. Shake and strain into your glass. Add a jalapeno slice as garnish

GOBLET OF FIRE

Prepare to experience bubbly excitement from this beautiful red drink. Once you take a sip, say whoever's name pops into your head. That's your champion for the Triwizard tournament!

INGREDIENTS

1 can of Sprite or 7-UP
A few drops of lime juice
2 tbsp grenadine syrup
3 maraschino cherries

PREPARATION:

1. Pour can of sprite into a glass
2. Add a few drops of lime juice to taste
3. Stir in 2 tbsp grenadine syrup
4. Add maraschino cherries on top
5. Enjoy!

HEALING POTION

If you ever have a sore throat or need a little added comfort during winter, this yummy and soothing tea is for you. Every sip will be magical!

INGREDIENTS

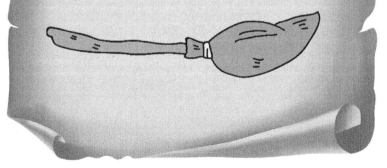

½ cup of lemonade
¾ cup of water
2 tbsp honey
one fruity tea bag of your choice (peach is fun)
one citrus mint tea bag

PREPARATION:

1. Bring the lemonade and water to a boil on the stove or in the microwave.
2. Add the tea bags and let them sit for as long as you would like.
3. Drizzle in the honey and stir.
4. Enjoy.

HUFFLEPUFF SMOOTHIE

Sweet and comforting, just like the Hufflepuffs. No one knows what Cedric Diggory's favorite drink was, but you can try this one and see if it would have qualified!

INGREDIENTS

1 cup frozen banana
½ cup frozen berries
½ cup of milk
1 tbsp nut butter
½ cup of yogurt

PREPARATION:

1. Add all ingredients to blender
2. Blend until smooth
3. Add water if more liquid is required
4. Pour into a cup and drink with a straw!

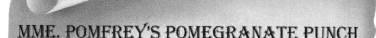

MME. POMFREY'S POMEGRANATE PUNCH

Give your guests a refreshing glass of punch at your next BBQ. Pomegranate juice on its own can be a little too sweet, but in a cocktail is immaculate. You'll be able to stay refreshed all day long.

INGREDIENTS

1 part pomegranate juice
1 part sparkling water
splash of cranberry juice
splash of orange juice

PREPARATION:

1. Prepare your cup or pitcher with ice.
2. Fill with equal parts pomegranate juice and sparkling water
3. Add splashes of cranberry juice and orange juice for extra flavor.
4. Drop cranberries and pomegranate seeds in the drink.
5. Place a thin orange wheel slice on the rim as garnish.

POLYJUICE POTION

Polyjuice potion looks and tastes better when it is used to imitate better people. Since you won't be shapeshifting for real (you can pretend), our version will taste better because of who is making it. Enjoy your yummy, beautiful drink!

INGREDIENTS

½ can of ginger ale
½ can of Sprite or 7-UP
1 scoop of lime sorbet
whipped cream
1 drop of food coloring, any color

PREPARATION:

1. Scoop your sorbet into a large glass.
2. Pour in your sprite, followed by ginger ale.
3. Add a drop of food colouring to your drink.
4. Top your drink with whipped cream.
5. Sip and enjoy.

PORTKEY-SICKNESS CURE

Flying through space whilst clutching a portkey can be a bit nauseating. If you feel woozy, try the Portkey-sickness cure. It'll help settle your stomach and clear your mind.

INGREDIENTS

1 cup ginger beer (non-alcoholic)
½ lime
¼ cup orange Fanta

PREPARATION:
1. Fill your glass with crushed ice.
2. Squeeze in half a lime with a juicer or your hand.
3. Pour in one cup of ginger beer.
4. Add ¼ cup orange Fanta for fruity flavor.
5. Use a lime wedge to garnish.
6. If you're in a car, just throw back some ginger beer. Ginger is an anti-inflammatory and will soothe your stomach.

PUMPKIN JUICE

If you've always wanted to know what pumpkin juice would taste like, now's your chance. Join your classmates in the great hall with this tasty classic. It'll feel the way hugging Harry, Ron, and Hermione would feel, but in your mouth.

INGREDIENTS

2 cups apple cider
½ cup pumpkin puree
½ tsp vanilla extract
1 tsp pumpkin pie spice
(whipped cream optional)

PREPARATION:

1. Place all ingredients in a blender. Mix.
2. Warm on the stove top if it's extra chilly outside. Drink as is or with ice if it needs some cooling.
3. Serve in a chilled glass for an icy treat.
4. Add a swirl of whipped cream and a pinch of pumpkin spice on top for extra garnish.

PUMPKIN JUICE SMOOTHIE

Finally, you get to try this Hogwarts staple for yourself! In smoothie form, no less.

INGREDIENTS

1 2/3 cups of pureed pumpkin
1/3 tsp pumpkin pie spice
1/3 tsp cinnamon
¼ cup brown sugar
1 1/3 cup orange juice
1 cup evaporated milk

PREPARATION:

1. Freeze orange juice in an ice cube tray.
2. Once frozen, place all ingredients in a blender and blend until smooth.

RUBEUS' RHUBARB REFRESHER

If you've always wanted to know what pumpkin juice would taste like, now's your chance. Join your classmates in the great hall with this tasty classic. It'll feel the way hugging Harry, Ron, and Hermione would feel, but in your mouth.

INGREDIENTS

2 ounces lime juice
splash of grenadine
3 dashes rhubarb bitters
sparkling water
rhubarb stalks

PREPARATION:

1. Add ice to your glass.
2. Squeeze in two ounces of lime juice.
3. Squirt three dashes of rhubarb bitters.
4. Fill with sparkling water.
5. Swirl grenadine on top.
6. Drop in a slice of rhubarb for garnish.

SNAPE SHAKE

This milkshake might be dark like Snape in all his broody glory, but it tastes delightful and light. A great pick-me-up or weekend treat.

INGREDIENTS

4 Oreo cookies
1 cup of milk
2 big scoops of vanilla ice cream
1 tbsp chocolate sauce

PREPARATION:

1. Place all Oreo cookies inside a Ziploc bag.
2. Crush the Oreo cookies with your hands or using a rolling pin.
3. Add the milk, ice cream and ¾ of the Oreo crumble to the blender.
4. Blend until smooth.
5. Pour into a glass and top with last Oreo cookie.

UMBRIDGE SHAKE

Dolores Umbridge is known for her pink outfits. Channel your inner Dolores while enjoying the pinkest drink of them all.

INGREDIENTS

2 handfuls of strawberries
½ cup of milk
2 scoops strawberry ice cream

PREPARATION:

1. Wash and cut up your strawberries.
2. Place strawberries, milk and ice cream in a blender.
3. Blend until smooth.
4. Pour into a glass and enjoy!

UNICORN BLOOD

This drink will not curse you. It will give you newfound excitement and enjoyment for all things magical.

INGREDIENTS

I can of sprite
A handful of blueberries

PREPARATION:

1. Ask an adult to help you puree the blueberries or mush them up in a bowl.
2. Scrape the blueberry puree into your glass.
3. Add sprite.
4. Enjoy your silvery blue unicorn blood.

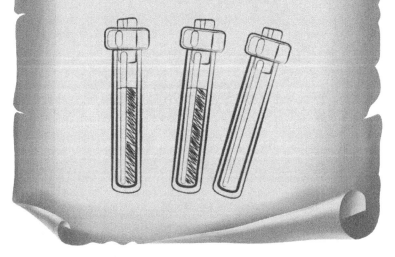

WATERMELON SUGAR

Not by Harry Potter, but by the other great Harry: Styles. The watermelon sugar drink will attract all Harrys to your vicinity. You're not Kendall Jenner yet, but you will be.

INGREDIENTS

1 seedless watermelon
½ cup lime juice
3 tbsp simple syrup
A can of sparkling water

PREPARATION:

1. Cut your watermelon into chunks and place them in a blender.
2. Add ½ a cup of lime juice and a can of sparkling water.
3. Make simple syrup with one part sugar to one part hot water. Stir. Pour three tablespoons into the blender.
4. Add some ice and blend until smooth.
5. Pour into champagne flutes and add a watermelon chunk on the rim as garnish.

Made in the USA
Monee, IL
19 November 2020